Julian Spalding

LOWRY

PHAIDON

To my parents

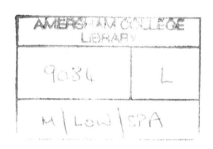

Phaidon Press Limited, Littlegate House, St Ebbe's Street, Oxford
Published in the United States of America by E. P. Dutton, New York

First published 1979

© *1979 by Phaidon Press Limited*

ISBN 0 7148 1996 4
Library of Congress Catalog Card Number: 79-50324

Printed in Great Britain by Morrison & Gibb Ltd, Edinburgh

LOWRY

This century has seen a breach open between contemporary art and the general public. Avant-garde, particularly abstract, art has been met with widespread incomprehension and abuse, and the art pundits have done little to allay the public's distrust. Lowry has both suffered and benefited from this division in taste: he has achieved a unique popularity with the general public, while to many in the art world his work still appears crude and vulgar, too easily accessible and spuriously commercial.

Lowry stands outside the mainstream development of modern British painting, partly because he had no desire to leave Manchester to work in London, and partly because the art world did not respond to his early overtures. He felt rejected, and his bitterness was perhaps reflected in the dogged way he chose to develop those aspects of his art which were guaranteed to offend refined aesthetic taste, his slapstick humour and his gauche simplicity of design. When in difficulties with a painting, Lowry preferred to ask the advice of someone completely untrained in art, rather than an expert. He gleaned a great deal from the paintings of children and amateurs – even, in one known instance, lifting a composition, *Boy with a Stomach-ache*, direct from a design by his friend, the amateur painter, the Reverend Geoffrey Bennett. Lowry provides a rare instance of a fully trained artist of genius choosing to develop his art, not in the atmosphere of mainstream artistic debate, but in the no less rigorous climate of popular opinion.

Lowry had an ambivalent attitude towards his isolated artistic position. He wanted the understanding and stimulus that could be gained from the company of other artists, yet he knew that the true direction of his art lay outside the main current of artistic opinion. After suffering a particularly fierce attack from the artist-critic Michael Ayrton, Lowry had the satisfaction of seeing a painting by himself fetch ten times the price of an Ayrton in the same auction. But popular success was not enough. Lowry's continual concern at the end of his life was 'Will I live? Will I live?' He wished earnestly to be remembered and judged as an artist, to know if his paintings would survive the test of time. The paradox of his position is summed up in his famous statement, recorded by Maurice Collis in 1951: 'My whole happiness and unhappiness were that my view was like nobody else's. Had it been like, I would not have been lonely, but had I not been lonely, I should not have seen what I did.' Predictably enough, commentators on Lowry have viewed him from the popular angle, concentrating on his personality rather than on his artistic achievement. The above quotation has been used, *ad nauseam*, to prove 'the loneliness of L. S. Lowry', when it in fact refers to Lowry's isolation as an artist rather than as a man. Had the alliteration not been quite so neat, it is doubtful if the phrase would have lingered. Lowry was not lonely, but a loner. He was a passionate individual who came to terms with his experience not by taking action but by detaching himself from life and spreading it before him in the operating theatre of his art.

Lowry was born in Old Trafford, Manchester, in 1887, and died a few miles away in Glossop in 1976. The industrial landscape of this northern conurbation circumscribed his whole life, but he lived long enough to see the sights of his youth – the gargantuan mills, the tapering chimneys, the rows of back-to-back terraces – give place to towering office-blocks and dual carriageways. His art can to some extent be seen as a final tribute to the Industrial Revolution, just as Constable's art had been a tribute to the pastoral English landscape just before it disappeared in the face of that same Revolution.

Lowry was the only child of middle-class parents. His father (Plate 1), who worked as a clerk in an estate agent's, had married, rather 'above himself', the daughter of a master hatter. There is no evidence that either of his parents was interested in painting; indeed, Lowry's father continued to disparage his son's efforts right up until his death in 1932. Lowry's mother seems to have been more sympathetic, however. She had established a considerable local reputation as a pianist and Lowry inherited from her, as well as her china and antique clocks, his lifelong passion for music. The family's finances, which were never substantial, gradually diminished, for Lowry's father, who devoted much of his time to charitable and cultural activities, paid little heed to his career at work or to his fortunes at home. When his son showed an interest in drawing, there seems to have been no question of his being able to attend the daytime sessions at the Manchester Municipal Art School, as these were too expensive; he had to content himself with evening classes. Immediately he left school at fifteen, Lowry had to earn his living as a clerk in an accountant's office, later transferring in 1910 to the Pall Mall Property Company, where he worked – first as a rent collector and clerk, later rising to Chief Cashier – until his retirement in 1952.

It came as a considerable surprise to the art world when it was discovered after his death in 1976 that Lowry had had a full-time job and had only been able to paint in the evenings and at weekends. His output had been of a size and standard worthy of any professional painter and it was well known that he was a slow worker, developing each picture gradually, often for at least a year. Moreover, Lowry himself had often said that he had painted full-time, having been supported, he claimed, by indulgent parents during their life and by his inheritance from them after their death. He was able to stage-manage this falsehood because he had always been a very private person and by the Second World War, when his work really began to become famous, he had lost many of his old acquaintances, and the few who remained were kept scrupulously apart in case they exchanged notes. Contradictory evidence, such as the *Manchester Evening News* article of 1933 which concluded 'Art for Mr Lowry is the antidote to a day of strain at a city desk', was, wherever possible, carefully suppressed. The reason behind this elaborate deception could be found in Lowry's increasing fear, as he grew older, of being dismissed as a 'Sunday painter', a mere untrained naïve. In fact, as he was at pains to tell commentators, he had attended art schools for twenty years, from 1905 to 1925, studying drawing in the life class. He did not emphasize the fact, however, that these studies were confined to evening class, five nights a week after work, at the comparatively low cost of seven shillings and sixpence a term.

In 1909 the Lowry family moved to Pendlebury. Though their home there was an ample semi-detached, the move marked a distinct fall in their social standing. Pendlebury was a lower-class, industrial suburb, much less convenient for the city centre where both Lowry and his father worked. Lowry's mother did not recover from her initial dislike of the place and she spent the last seven years of her life as a recluse, never leaving the house. Lowry, however, with the artist's alchemy, turned this base metal into gold. 'At first I disliked it. After a year I got used to it. Within a few years I began to be interested and at length I became obsessed by it and painted nothing else for thirty years.' His chronology is accurate. By 1912 he had drawn his first mill-worker, by 1915 he was designing complete mill scenes, and by 1920 his drawing style had been successfully transferred into oils.

With a disregard for fact that we have come to expect from him, Lowry later concertina'd his gradual growth of interest in the industrial scene into a momentary revelation. To John Rothenstein, the Director of the Tate, he attributed the moment of vision to an enforced wait on Pendlebury Station in 1916, when he suddenly saw a distant mill spill out its employees. To another commentator, he claimed that the revelation came to him while standing in Stumps Park a year earlier, in 1915: 'I was with a man and he said look and there I saw it. It changed my life. From then on I devoted myself to it.' Both statements undoubtedly contain some grain of truth; they were perhaps but two instances in a sequence of revelations that constituted the unveiling of Lowry's vision of the industrial scene. With five nights a week devoted to academic drawing, Lowry had only the weekends free to develop a more personal style, and it is hardly surprising that his 'vision' grew slowly and hesitatingly over a period of fifteen years.

Lowry's early drawings in the life class were bold and vigorous. He drew clearly, defining the shapes and planes as simple areas bound together by bold, black outlines. Something of the quality of these drawings can be seen in his *Self Portrait* (Plate 18), one of the few paintings that Lowry executed from the life. The picture has suffered from damp and lost much of its colour, but one can still appreciate the rhythmic arrangement of the simplified shapes that make up the composition: the arching peak of the cap, balanced by the curves of his collars, the clean line of the jaw, and the firm eyes and mouth. It is a portrait of a dedicated young painter intent on his trade.

Lowry reveals a very different personality when he is drawing or painting from his imagination. It is difficult to date his early drawings, but as well as the academic nudes and portraits there are a number of highly finished crowd scenes showing people gathered on beaches, in parks, or in the street. Their style is different from that of his products in the life class; it is zany and angular, and reminds one strongly of popular comic-strip or postcard illustrations. Lowry recognized his need for the discipline of his academic studies, but he was already independent enough to know that his true style lay outside artistic convention, in the world of popular culture. Many of these elaborate drawings were composed from memory, from brief notes he had made on his journeys as a rent collector or on the regular walks he used to take every Saturday night from Pendlebury to Bolton. He chose Saturday nights because they were the time of most activity in the streets. Lowry's paintings do not show the inside of the mills, they do not show the mill-hand at work (this is, incidentally, the reason why they have been dismissed by the politically motivated painters of the seventies as 'reactionary'). His art is the art of the public place. Everything depicted in his paintings can be seen by a passer-by, by an outsider, like Lowry himself. But he is most interested of all when a personal and private event surfaces amid a crowd of strangers, disrupting the public calm (as in Plates 9, 13, 17 and 47).

Walking, looking, and then working at home became Lowry's regular pattern of activity. 'I never paint on the spot, but look for a long time, make drawings and think.' However much they may appear so, Lowry's paintings are not straight portraits of the mill scenes of Lancashire. 'I liked in those days', Lowry said, 'to do a picture entirely out of my mind's eye, straight onto the canvas. It was difficult to start, but you put something down, add to it, and suddenly you find you've put in some very nice things and you're going along very well. . . . Oh, I liked that, to do a picture out of my own head on the blank canvas. I think it gets nearer the truth, because there are no facts to hamper you, and you are setting down something that comes entirely from your own imagination.' One has only to glance through this book to see how many times the same lamp-posts, chimneys, mills and figures reappear. Each of his pictures is, in fact, an imaginary composite of a number of different scenes created out of the characters and stage props of his drama. His paintings are like stage sets; his mills (Plate 7) slide into position like flats, while his little figures remind one of those cut-out cardboard figures that slip back and forth on metal rods in Victorian toy theatres.

Lowry had a great love for the theatre. Any Saturday afternoon, when it was too wet for drawing, he would go to see a play or visit a music-hall. James Fitton, the painter who studied with Lowry at evening classes, recalled how once they went together to see Fred Karno's 'Mumming Birds' – a company in which that other great master of little men, Charlie Chaplin, had performed. At least one play, Stanley Houghton's *Hindle Wakes*, had a direct influence on the development of Lowry's art. It was one of the first plays to deal realistically with the lives of the working-class families who lived in the Lancashire mill towns, and when Lowry saw it in 1912 he could not get it out of his mind. The stage directions for the opening scene read: 'Through the window can be seen the darkening day. Against the sky an outline of roof-tops and chimneys.' One could almost be looking, with hindsight, at an early Lowry.

However much the theatre may have opened Lowry's eyes to the richness of the industrial life around him, it is doubtful whether he would have realized its possibilities as a source of subject-matter sufficient to sustain a lifetime's career as a painter, had it not been for the precedent set by the paintings of his drawing master at night-school, Adolphe Valette. This French artist had arrived in Manchester in 1904 or –5. Familiar with Impressionism, he soon saw the pictorial possibilities of the all-pervasive Manchester mist. He made small oil studies of urban scenes while standing in the street, with his paintbox supported by a strap that went round his neck, holding a small panel or canvas in the lid. These little paintings are in the true Impressionist style, delightful atmospheric studies painted with a multi-coloured array of spontaneous brushstrokes. Between 1909 and 1913 Valette attempted the industrial scene on a grander scale. For these large street scenes he abandoned the Impressionist style and employed a more studied technique, building up his pictures by means of carefully aligned vertical strokes that give the impression that the mist is perpetually drizzling. The buildings fade rapidly into the distance, and the figures too – whether pedestrians, cabmen or men pushing carts – are reduced to dark silhouettes that pale as they recede into the mist. Though Valette refused to teach Lowry to paint (he maintained that only drawing could be taught), the younger artist must have learnt a great deal from the example of these paintings. He often used the same short, vertical brushstroke, but with greater variety (see Plate 21), and used many of the same street props. What is lacking in Valette's paintings, however, is the sense of occasion, the moment of dramatic tension that inspired and bound together so many of Lowry's pictures.

'Accidents interest me', Lowry once commented; 'I've a very queer mind you know. What fascinates me is the people they attract, the patterns these people form and the atmosphere of tension when something has happened.' *Sudden Illness* (1920; Plate 17) is one of the very first of Lowry's paintings to reveal his mature style. A small crowd has gathered on an exposed strip of road. There is hardly any warmth in the picture except for a lingering golden tint in the sky. The subject itself is enough to send a chill through the viewer. The cold air breathes on the faces of the passers-by who stand around the collapsed invalid, who lies isolated from them by his illness. A dark cloud spreads overhead; a hush seems to have descended on the waiting crowd. The thought that the sick man might die crosses one's mind. This feeling of a tense moment of stillness has been created by Lowry's control of the composition. The picture has been arranged according to the laws of the golden section, that classical division of the rectangle into harmoniously related parts. The sick man has fallen at the intersection of the golden mean, the vertical division being indicated by the black cloud, the horizontal by the lower edge of the dark wall. The black gap that marks the sick man's position is exactly complemented, both compositionally and emotively, by the grey smoke that spreads into the air from the distant factory chimney. The figures walking in from either side, too, have their place, because they concentrate one's attention on the centre. On the right a man turns to look at us, but he is too far away to involve us in the scene, he merely observes us observing him. Lowry always stands back from his pictures. In fact there is often a bar running across the bottom of his paintings (see Plates 28, 33 and 39) which marks the edge of the stage, dividing the viewer from the scene. This feeling of distance is not symbolic of Lowry's 'lone-liness', of his isolation from other people, but reflects the element in his make-up that allowed him to stand back and see the world from a fresh viewpoint. Only by doing so could he see the patterns these crowds formed, and grasp their significance.

During the twenties, Lowry produced a remarkable series of paintings that combine his chosen subject with a strong feeling for the traditional aesthetic values of harmony and order. He was still, at this point in his career, hoping to establish himself as a professional painter, to find acceptance in the art world. With hindsight we can see that his work of this period is in close harmony with the paintings of the Camden Town Group (especially the work of Ginner, Drummond and Bevan), who had gathered round Sickert in his London studio. The emphatic outlines, the silhou-etted architecture, the thick, encrusted paint and stylized figures are features common to both their and Lowry's work. This is not so surprising as it may seem at first, since they shared the ancestry of Impressionism and had both developed their treatment of the urban landscape out of an attempt to absorb the influence of the Post-Impressionists, particularly Van Gogh, Seurat and Cézanne. In this context Lowry's art does not seem such an isolated phenomenon. When it is remembered that the twenties saw a widespread reaction to the experiments in abstraction carried out before the War and witnessed a return to representational art, then Lowry's art can be seen to be even more in keeping with the spirit of his times. His art takes its place quite naturally alongside William Roberts's clockwork robots and Stanley Spencer's figurative conglomerations.

Lowry's magnificent paintings of the twenties rely for their effect mainly on the careful disposition of vertical and horizontal features. Rising mill walls, tapering chimneys, lamp-posts and figures complement the flat roofs, rows of terraces, and roads lined with curbs and tramways. As in *Sudden Illness*, the features are often disposed according to the laws of the golden section. Plates 7, 8, 11, 12, 13, 16, 17 and 21 form the impressive group of works that have in common an off-centre focal point, placed at the intersection of the golden mean. The centre of interest is invariably a crowd, gathered round an incident (often tragic) or, in some, merely spilling out from a gateway. It is interesting to note that one of the few curved features that regularly recur in these paintings is the homely arch that caps each erupting exit. In *Northern Hospital* (Plate 10), surely one of Lowry's masterpieces, the crowd has been pushed to the extreme left, while the pivot of the picture is the vacant arch on the right, pierced by the black mast that defines the position of the golden mean. A similar vacant arch sustains the composition in *Peel Park, Salford* (Plate 4). Through it can be seen the row of red terraces which became a regular feature of Lowry's art at this time (see Plate 13). In both *Northern Hospital* and *Peel Park, Salford* the hollow arch filled with light serves to offset the huge mass of the dark buildings.

The grandeur of these early paintings is due largely to Lowry's grasp of scale, his ability to embrace the vast and the minute, both mass and movement, in one encompassing design. In *St Augustine's Church, Pendlebury* (Plate 14) Lowry has emphasized the towering mass of the church by placing it in the centre, its sides tapering in as it recedes up into the sky, dwarfing the white graves and the path at its feet. A similar sense of the colossal inspired his later paintings of ships entering harbours, while his painting *South Shields* (Plate 36) depends for its impact on the relationship between the large boats at the wharf with their towering prows, and the busy little tugs at water level. In the early pastel *Coming from the Mill* (Plate 6) the mill walls rise up the sides of the picture like dark cliffs. The figures do not disturb the scene, they are as still as the dark gaps in the curtained windows. The only movement in the picture is the smoke drifting in the distance. Lowry's achievement in the twenties was to activate his figures and thereby add a new dimension to the scene. In *Coming Out of School* (Plate 11), for example, the movement of the children and the drift of the smoke perfectly complement the still weight of the architecture. Though his paintings of this period embrace humorous incidents, these remain only details in his overriding scheme of aesthetic harmony.

Coming from the Mill (1930; Plate 7) marks a change in Lowry's work. The sombre mood of the earlier pastel (Plate 6) has been dispelled by brighter, busier colours bounded by black outlines. One could almost be watching a mechanical stage set. Suddenly a bell sounds: it is five o'clock; the mill opens its doors, and the city springs to life. In *The Arrest* (1925; Plate 19) a note of humour is struck by the apt name of the street, but the grey tones and regimented design damp any potential gaiety in this grim scene in which Lowry himself could easily have been involved as a rent collector. The picture is a cruel rather than comic exposure of the incident. *A Fight* (Plate 24), painted ten years later, uses the same set but from closer in. Here again, in the thirties, we can observe changes occurring in his style. The tones have become brighter, the colours and lines aggressively crude. The squat arch of the door describes the arc that the fellow's arms must have taken as he rammed the hat about his opponent's ears. The composition takes its cue from the slapstick comedy of the strip cartoon or music-hall. Lowry here is turning away from classical design to a wilful naïvety, from the aesthetic towards more popular forms of expression.

One can only surmise the reasons for this change in his art. Lowry himself felt that he had been rejected by the art world and he therefore may well have decided to abandon those aspects of his art that would appeal to the aesthetes, and to commit himself wholeheartedly to an exploration of the popular. Perhaps his rejection by the art world served only as a catalyst or reagent to speed up a natural development in his art. The art world had not, by any standards, rejected him completely. Lowry was well known in Manchester, and his few exhibited works had received good reviews in the *Guardian*. In 1930 Manchester City Art Gallery bought its first Lowry, *An Accident* (Plate 13), and the following year the Tate bought *Coming out of School* (Plate 11). Lowry, moreover, had had paintings regularly accepted at the Salon d'Automne in Paris from 1928 to 1933 and had the honour of being included *and* illustrated in Edouard Joseph's *Dictionnaire Biographique des Artistes Contemporains 1910–1930*. Such successes were considerable but sporadic; they did not bring him enough income to support himself as a full-time professional painter.

The thirties proved a critical time, too, in Lowry's home life. His father died in 1932, followed, seven years later, by his mother, after a long and painful illness. Lowry found he had much less time for painting. He was wearied by his work and by the long hours spent nursing his mother, and his paintings became introspective and highly symbolic. He began a series of imaginary staring heads, based on self-portraits, which express both his anguish and his exhaustion. They can be interpreted as an analysis of his relationship with his parents. The one illustrated here, *Head of a Boy in a Yellow Jacket* (1935; Plate 25), less obviously violent than some, is one of the most profound of the series. The eyes and mouth, large ears and outsize collar express the earnest innocence and anxious loneliness of a child who might well have lost his parents. It is difficult for an artist, even one working in a suburb of Manchester, to escape the spirit of his age, and I think these racked heads are not unrelated to the new wave of figurative expressionism that was beginning to flood through Paris and other capitals of the art world. It is not unconstructive to compare Lowry's more extreme portraits with the new style of the figurative expressionists, with the sado-masochistic paintings of Francis Bacon, though these are, of course, on quite a different scale. The curtain of falling paint behind Lowry's heads, like Bacon's satanic showers, gives these paintings their sense of despairing finality.

Vertical lines can, however, be read as either rising or falling, hopeful or despairing. In one remarkable and isolated painting of the thirties, *St John's Church, Manchester* (1938; Plate 27), Lowry came to terms with his bitterness, resolving it in paint. The picture is as severely symmetrical as his portraits. Its secret lies in the subtle movement of the brushstrokes, those same parallel strokes that Lowry had inherited from his master Valette. The sky appears to descend as the tower rises, yet the horizontal brushmarks on the church's façade reassert its weighty presence in the misty air. The downward movement through the flanking houses and the recession of the road serve as a crucible for the ambivalent movement in the centre. Expansion and contraction, descent and ascent have been embraced in one composition to strike a note of serenity in one of the most troubled passages of Lowry's life.

The Second World War was a demoralizing experience for many artists, and Lowry has left us one monument to its tragic absurdity in his painting *An Island* (1942; Plate 29). It is particularly poignant to compare it with *Market Scene, Northern Town* (Plate 28), painted in 1939 before the War had begun to bite. A similar building stands in the centre of both pictures. One is surrounded by a sea of activity (the haze of the white under the awning floats behind *and* in front of the house), the other by a scene of desolation. *An Island* is surely not an image of Lowry's loneliness, as has often been suggested. If it were, the house should be a living symbol in the heart of the ruin. But it is not alive; its windows are black, the door swings open on the hinge. The house is as dead and empty as the wrecked land around it. What life there is in the picture creeps back at the edges, surrounding the island of desolation with its freak survivor in the centre, an ironical joke on the part of death.

After the War, Lowry's art regained its momentum. In 1939 he had been given his first one-man exhibition in London by Alex McNeill Reid, who had happened to see his pictures at a framer's. The venture was a great success; sixteen paintings were sold, including one to the Tate (Plate 15), and from then on Lowry's future seemed assured. In 1948 he finally left the house in Pendlebury where his parents had died and moved to Mottram-in-Longendale, a particularly bleak village on the edge of the Peak, near Glossop. He detested the place, but the move was followed by a remarkable burst of activity. By 1950 he had painted a number of very large canvases – *The Pond* (Plate 34), *Open Space* (Plate 32), *Lake Landscape* (Plate 35) and *The Cripples* (see Plate 42 for its later version) – and had thereby established the major themes that were to occupy him for the next twenty years. His style had once more begun to change. *The Pond* no longer depends on a balance of horizontal and vertical features (they are still there, but play a secondary role – witness the ridiculously tall telegraph poles). The huge panorama is now held together by the curves that flow through the composition, bending the terraces and sinking the centre of the horizon. The brushstrokes are no longer aligned vertically or horizontally, but swell and flow with the forms they describe. In the background the towers, chimneys, spires and roofs rise up from and sink back into the welter of white. Lowry has reverted to the free, impressionistic handling of his earliest studies, such as the beautifully sensitive portrait of his father (Plate 1), painted in 1910, or the *Sailing Boats* (Plate 22), which was painted specially at his mother's request to remind her of the holidays the family had spent at Lytham St Anne's.

As Lowry regains his self-confidence, it is not surprising to find him returning to a freer, more spontaneous style of brushwork. He was a natural painter, as his early portrait of his father proves, and he enjoyed a style that gave him ample room to experiment and display his skills. As his understanding of character deepened and his grasp of technique grew stronger, his simplifications became bolder and more daring. In the bottom right-hand corner of the painting *In a Park* (Plate 42) an old man stoops over a cane. It is difficult to see how Lowry has created such a lively expression out of five smudges of paint, without even indicating a mouth. In *Man Drinking Water* (Plate 47) a minimal face has been created out of the tail-end of the brushstrokes, yet it presents a perfect picture of rejection and humiliation. Lowry enjoyed above all the malleability of paint; a small inflection of the brush could bring a smile to a face, another could as easily wipe it away. Again it is the sense of theatre in Lowry that comes to the surface. He liked the Restoration dramatists because they 'managed a little world of puppets – pull a string and this one jumps'. 'I can't do a cat yet', he remarked in 1960. 'The only way I can do a cat is by doing a very bad dog and then in a way decapitating it and it becomes a cat.' Lowry was the master of his little painted world: he may have filled it with images of human foibles and suffering, but there is no trace of sentiment, and he ruled it, like a Greek god, with playful malice.

One of the most startling features of Lowry's later work is his use of pure white backgrounds, which serve equally for grass, air, tarmac and sky. This white is not snow; it is too hard, and does not lie on the roofs or window-sills. It is entirely artificial. Its origin lies in the naturally misty atmosphere of the Manchester basin, a mist that diffuses the light, smothers shadows and rapidly subdues all features except those nearest to the eye. Valette had been fascinated by it, but he painted it with the grey, blue and rose palette of an Impressionist. Already by 1920, in *Sudden Illness* (Plate 17), Lowry had observed that pavements and roads often reflect the light of the sky, making the figures on them appear dark silhouettes. In *The Bandstand* (Plate 3), the restrained pinks, greens and greys are the colours of an overcast day, but the bandstand roof has been painted white because it reflects the sky. It is no great leap from this to Lowry's rendering of the awnings in *Market Scene, Northern Town* (Plate 28), except that the white has now become artificially bright. Lowry himself attributed his use of white to a criticism levelled at his work in 1921 by Bernard Taylor, the *Guardian* critic. He told Lowry that his pictures were too dark and needed to be brighter so that they would 'stand out against the wall' (it was fashionable then to have dark interiors). Lowry claimed that, in anger, he painted a couple of figures on a pure white background and was surprised to find that Taylor liked them. This has all the ingredients of a typical Lowry story, a tactical oversimplification designed to divert the listener. Lowry had already painted *Sudden Illness* a year before this criticism, and two years previously had painted the seminal *Pit Tragedy* (Plate 5), in which a thick white serves for both sky and ground. It is needed here to offset the gloomy depths of the main colours; though in this case the white may have been heightened later, for Lowry habitually retouched his paintings.

These pure white backgrounds enabled Lowry to concentrate on the figures. He had come to realize that 'the interest in the pictures was in the figures and I had to keep them artificially white because the picture was worthless if the ground and the figures merged'. By the late fifties he had begun to feel more strongly about his figures than he had about his 'vision of the industrial scene'. He said of the *Two Brothers* (1960; Plate 41) that 'it is absolutely symbolic of life; there are those two little fellows, they could be brother salesmen, they could be calling door-to-door collecting insurance . . . there's the church at the back there, two kids there, and these two poor devils going about their business. Now that's the industrial scene too.' In many of his paintings at this time, the industrial scene itself recedes into the background, leaving the figures isolated in a sea of white. In *In a Park* (1963; Plate 42) the factory chimneys in the distance bleed into the disturbed white paint. Each figure hangs suspended in its own allotted space. Shadows here would be as superfluous and distracting as they would be in a Russian icon. The white in Lowry's pictures, like the gold in an icon, represents light and space. It is the ether of his imaginary world. Almost every character in the painting is bent out of true in some way. The figures create a delightful pattern, albeit of funny walks. When asked why he was so fascinated by cripples, Lowry replied simply: 'they are so *comic*'. The pains he took to follow them and draw them (once he counted ninety cripples on one journey between Mottram and Bury) suggest a rather morbid curiosity. But it is possibly Lowry's childlike frankness of vision that offends those of us who are used to ignoring politely any deviation from the norm. Isolated from life by their oddity, these physical freaks are perfect subjects for Lowry's clinical world. Exposed on his bare white canvases, the tragicomedy of their existence is highlighted. Partially cut off in real life, when portrayed by the artist as completely isolated they become very much alive. By the sixties Lowry had become fascinated by what he called 'the battle of life', by those individuals who had suffered 'some great tragedy that has occurred in their lives and has arisen because they were not proof to stand up against such a calamity'; or, as George Orwell described them in *Down and Out in Paris and London* (1933), those 'people who had fallen into solitary, half-mad grooves of life'. The man drinking water portrayed in Plate 47 was seen by Lowry in a public lavatory in Piccadilly Gardens, Manchester, where he sidled up to a tap, and, after glancing round, drew a tin can from under his coat and filled it at the spout. *The Beggar* (Plate 46) relies for its impact on the simplified shapes made by the repeated curves, the lowered head and raised arm, that so well express his degraded humility.

These pictures arouse in us the contrasting feelings of pity and of fun, although they have been painted with a seering objectivity. Lowry needed to stand apart to see things clearly, for what they really were. This heightened objectivity, so crucial to the artist, is actually quite a common experience. One has only to stop for a moment in a busy high street to notice the movement of the crowd, the legs scissoring along the pavement, the idlers standing around, suitcase salesmen, stray dogs – all the ingredients, in fact, of a Lowry picture. Only by standing apart in this way and keeping still could Lowry create such lively scenes as *Good Friday, Daisy Nook* (Plate 33), a remarkable evocation of childhood memories of a fair; the rhythms and patterns in the crowd are extremely complex, though they break down in the distance where the crowd looks as if it has been blasted by a shotgun over the hillside. In *The Pond* (Plate 34) the life of the scene is spread far beneath us; we are given a mind's-eye view. In Lowry's very last mill painting, *Industrial Scene with Monument* (Plate 48), executed in 1972, the little figures have been incised with a sharp knife so that they stand out from the white ground. Nowhere has Lowry created such an effect of movement as in the hurried interweaving of people beneath the statelier rhythms set up by the rows of white mill windows. Amidst it all stands a tall black monument. When Mervyn Levy asked him the meaning of the picture, Lowry replied: 'Well, Sir, I suppose you can say that the monument is me! That's all I am now, you know. A monument to myself! What a way to end up.' Standing apart from life and viewing things objectively can result in impotence. Perhaps it is not too Freudian to suggest that this last image of Lowry's isolation has, by some odd trick of the unconscious, been transformed into its opposite, the time-honoured symbol of potent involvement, around which the movement cascades.

It is difficult to make a convincing interpretation of art in terms of psychology alone. Lowry was a secretive person and little is known about his personal life. But his fierce drawing *Courting* (1955; Plate 43) can surely be interpreted as an ironic joke at his own expense. The idiocy of the situation draws from us an almost involuntary gut-laugh; the experience is by no means unique to the artist. The old man with his knees together has little hope of the girl. But does he want her? His series of heads of Anne (Plate 40) clearly express a fascination with this mysterious young ballet dancer who came to visit him from nowhere in an expensive limousine. The graceful line of her hair as it flows down the nape of her neck, the tilt of her face, reveal his affection for her; but the metallic parting of her hair, the staring eyes and pursed mouth suggest that Lowry is in the process of transforming her into an icon of the ideal girl, transfixing her in art. It is not, perhaps, coincidental that Lowry was at that time buying his collection of Rossetti's stylized female heads. He found them, he said, 'very unpleasant but very fascinating'. Their obsessive formalization is not so far from the spirit of his own work. Lowry fettered his most personal themes in extremely tight straitjackets. His series of anguished self-portraits (Plate 25), like his portraits of Anne, stare straight over us like ancient Egyptian gods. They have been severed from life by self-analysis, shorn of sentiment by a ruthless symmetry.

The horizontal bar already mentioned that appears at the foot of so many of Lowry's canvases, as in Plates 28, 33 and 39, for example, became in Lowry's later work not just a barrier dividing the spectator from the stage, but a natural complement to the vertical; it represents a rest from activity, or from life. *Man Lying on a Wall* (Plate 39) was developed from an incident Lowry saw from a train window. A tired businessman had taken an unconventional rest on a wall. Lowry has inscribed his own initials on the suitcase; he himself might have been tempted to take such a rest. He had, moreover, similarly embellished a coffin in a little funeral picture painted by his friend Geoffrey Bennett. The man's hat lies on his chest. Could it be his last rites? The spire points up, the black umbrella points down. Has Lowry in fact laid himself to rest, in a rather unconventional position, in his own industrial landscape? In Salford Art Gallery, which houses the finest public collection of Lowry's work, there is a tiny painting called *Waiting for the Tide*. A long barge lies on the water, just like this gent on the wall, its prow, like his boots, pointing up to heaven. The tide it waits for, the rising white sea, is surely an image of impending death.

Water appears regularly throughout Lowry's art as a flat feature devoid of everything except the sky's reflection. In *An Accident* (Plate 13), though we are told the victim drowned in a near-by canal, we cannot help associating the strip of stagnant water in the bottom right-hand corner with the tragedy. In *An Island* (Plate 29) the water covers the scars of a ravaged land, in *Lake Landscape* (Plate 35) it has flooded the earth, and in *The Sea* (Plate 37) we are back to the second day of the Creation. The white above and the white below are divided by a hairbreadth horizontal line that fades to nothing in the centre. Lowry's imaginative ether, in which he isolates the objects of his art, has itself become the subject of his pictures, the image of an immense void. His seascapes may well have been painted as an antidote to the activity of his mill scenes; but although they can be interpreted more as a relief than a threat, these vast empty spaces are never quite free from a funereal shiver.

Lowry died in 1976. He had reached his eighty-ninth year, but during the last five of them he had aged rapidly and had practically given up painting, only drawing a little for children. At his funeral many of his friends met each other for the first time. Lowry had always kept them carefully apart, partly because he feared they might discover too much about him, and partly because he liked to remain the centre of each one's attention. He used to visit them mainly at weekends; after his parents died he always had the problem of where to get his Sunday lunch, for he never cooked for himself. Lowry often remarked that he would like to be consciously present at his own funeral. He imagined that no one would be there, except for the solicitor of course, and he would be wondering if he could 'get away to catch his two-thirty'. 'Well,' Lowry would add, 'why *shouldn't* he catch his two-thirty?' He saw no earthly reason why life should not go on.

Lowry liked anything that exhibited an independent life of its own. The fat robin in Plate 45 is a funny, ungainly ball of feathers that is so intent on something it has seen away to the left (probably a worm) that it has absolutely no time for its creator, or the rest of us. Margo Ingham-Drake, the Manchester gallery director who supported Lowry for so many years, recalled how he used to engage in staring matches with her dachshund, whom he found extremely comical, until there was 'either a salvo of barking . . . or a great roar of laughter from Lowry, according to which one of them won'. Lowry liked anything that showed enough spirit to fight back, including cripples offended by his perpetual staring. The figures in his pictures are isolated not because they are pathetic or lonely, but because they are alive and independent. It is Lowry's unquenchable spirit of fun that gives his paintings their bright, audacious presence. In his pictures, though he claimed he painted nothing but 'gloom', life always springs back again, no matter how tough the battle.

Outline Biography

1887	Born 1 November, Old Trafford, Manchester, only son of R. S. M. Lowry (estate agent's clerk) and Elizabeth Hobson (accomplished pianist).
1904	Joined Thomas Aldred & Son, Chartered Accountants, as a clerk.
1905–15	Attended evening classes at Manchester Municipal School of Art, studying in the life class under Adolphe Valette.
1909	Moved to 117 Station Road, Pendlebury, with his parents.
1910–52	Worked as rent collector and clerk with the Pall Mall Property Co., Manchester.
1915–25	Irregular attendance at evening classes at Salford School of Art.
1921	Exhibition in offices of the Manchester architect Roland Thomasson. Sold his first picture, *The Lodging House* (Plate 8).
1925	Exhibited with the Manchester Society of Modern Painters.
1927–36	Exhibited regularly with the New English Art Club.
1928–33	Regularly accepted by the Salon d'Automne, Paris.
1930	Manchester City Art Gallery purchased *An Accident* (Plate 13).
1931	The Tate Gallery purchased *Coming out of School* (Plate 11).
1932	Death of Lowry's father in February. Exhibited for the first time at the Manchester Academy of Fine Arts and at the Royal Academy, London.
1934	Elected member of the Royal Society of British Artists.
1939	First one-man exhibition at the Lefèvre Gallery, London. Death of Lowry's mother in October.
1941	One-man exhibition at Salford City Art Gallery.
1948	Moved to The Elms, 23 Stalybridge Road, Mottram-in-Longdendale, Cheshire.
1952	Retired on full pension.
1955	Elected Associate of the Royal Academy.
1959	Retrospective exhibition, Manchester City Art Gallery.
1962	Elected Royal Academician.
1966–7	Arts Council touring retrospective exhibition.
1970	Refused knighthood.
1976	Died 23 February at Woods Hospital, Glossop, after an attack of pneumonia.

Select Bibliography

Andrews, Allen, *The Life of L. S. Lowry*. London, Jupiter Books, 1977.

Collis, Maurice, *The Discovery of L. S. Lowry*. London, Alex Reid & Lefèvre, 1951.

Levy, Mervyn, *L. S. Lowry*. London, Studio Books ('Painter of Today' series), 1961.

Levy, Mervyn, *Drawings of L. S. Lowry*. London, Covy, Adams & Mackay, 1963, and Jupiter Books, 1973.

Levy, Mervyn, *The Paintings of L. S. Lowry, oils and watercolour*. London, Jupiter Books, 1975.

Levy, Mervyn, *L. S. Lowry RA 1887–1976*. London, Royal Academy of Arts, 1976.

Martin, Sandra, *A Pre-Raphaelite Passion: The Private Collection of L. S. Lowry*. Manchester City Art Galleries, 1977.

Martin, Sandra, *Adolphe Valette 1876–1942*. Manchester City Art Galleries, 1976.

McLean, David, *L. S. Lowry*. London, The Medici Society, 1978.

Mullineaux, Frank, *L. S. Lowry: The Salford Collection*. Salford Art Gallery, 1977.

Mullins, Edward, *L. S. Lowry: Catalogue of the Retrospective Exhibition*. Arts Council of Great Britain, 1966.

Rothenstein, John, *Modern English Painters, Vol. II*. London, Eyre & Spottiswoode, 1956.

List of Plates

1. *Portrait of the Artist's Father.* 1910. Canvas, 41 × 31 cm. Salford Museum and Art Gallery.

2. *Fishing Boats at Lytham.* 1915. Pastel, 40 × 50.2 cm. Collection of Mrs Phyllis Bloom.

3. *Bandstand, Peel Park, Salford.* 1928. Board, 29.2 × 39.2 cm. Salford Museum and Art Gallery.

4. *Peel Park, Salford.* 1927. Board, 35 × 50 cm. Salford Museum and Art Gallery.

5. *Pit Tragedy.* 1919. Canvas, 39.3 × 49.5 cm. Collection of the Revd. Geoffrey S. Bennett.

6. *Coming from the Mill.* c.1917–18. Pastel, 43.7 × 56.1 cm. Salford Museum and Art Gallery.

7. *Coming from the Mill.* 1930. Canvas, 42 × 52 cm. Salford Museum and Art Gallery.

8. *The Lodging House.* 1921. Pastel, 48.9 × 30.5 cm. Salford Museum and Art Gallery.

9. *A Quarrel.* 1935. Canvas, 53 × 39.5 cm. Collection of Mr Michael Spring.

10. *Northern Hospital.* 1926. Panel, 43.2 × 51.4 cm. Private Collection.

11. *Coming out of School.* 1927. Plywood, 34.3 × 51.1 cm. London, Tate Gallery.

12. *The Funeral.* 1928. Board, 34.3 × 46 cm. Collection of Mr Monty Bloom.

13. *An Accident.* 1926. Panel, 36.3 × 61 cm. Manchester City Art Galleries.

14. *St Augustine's Church, Pendlebury.* 1920. Oil, 33.6 × 52.1 cm. Collection of the Revd. Geoffrey S. Bennett.

15. *Dwellings, Ordsall Lane, Salford.* 1927. Plywood, 43.1 × 53.3 cm. London, Tate Gallery.

16. *Returning from Work.* 1929. Canvas, 43.2 × 61 cm. Private Collection.

17. *Sudden Illness.* 1920. Canvas, 34.3 × 54.6 cm. Collection of Mr M. D. H. Bloom.

18. *Self-Portrait.* 1925. Board, 56.5 × 47 cm. Salford Museum and Art Gallery.

19. *The Arrest.* 1927. Canvas, 53.4 × 43.2 cm. Nottingham Castle Museum and Art Gallery.

20. *Whit Week Procession at Swinton.* 1921. Panel, 30.5 × 45.7 cm. Private Collection.

21. *Going to the Match.* 1931. Panel, 25.3 × 47 cm. Collection of the Revd. Geoffrey S. Bennett.

22. *Sailing Boats.* 1930. Board, 35.6 × 45.7 cm. The L. S. Lowry Estate.

23. *The Artist's Bedroom, Pendlebury.* 1940. Canvas, 35.8 × 51.2 cm. Salford Museum and Art Gallery.

24. *A Fight.* 1935. Canvas, 53.2 × 39.5 cm. Salford Museum and Art Gallery.

25. *Head of a Boy in a Yellow Jacket.* 1935. Canvas, 50.8 × 40.8 cm. Collection of Mr M. D. H. Bloom.

26. *Landscape in Wigan.* 1925. Canvas, 34.3 × 34 cm. Private Collection.

27. *St John's Church, Manchester.* 1938. Plywood, 30.5 × 29.2 cm. Collection of the Revd. Geoffrey S. Bennett.

28. *Market Scene, Northern Town.* 1939. Canvas, 45.7 × 61.1 cm. Salford Museum and Art Gallery.

29. *An Island.* 1942. Canvas, 45.6 × 60.9 cm. Manchester City Art Galleries.

30. *A Street Scene, St Simon's Church.* 1928. Board, 45.7 × 38.1 cm. Salford Museum and Art Gallery.

31. *After the Blitz.* 1942. Board, 52.1 × 41.9 cm. Private Collection.

32. *Open Space.* 1950. Canvas, 76.2 × 101.6 cm. London, Crane Kalman Gallery.

33. *Good Friday, Daisy Nook.* 1946. Canvas, 76.2 × 101.6 cm. Private Collection.

34. *The Pond.* 1950. Canvas, 114.3 × 152.4 cm. London, Tate Gallery.

35. *Lake Landscape.* 1950. Canvas, 71.1 × 91.4 cm. University of Manchester, Whitworth Art Gallery.

36. *South Shields.* 1962. Canvas, 76.2 × 101.6 cm. London, Crane Kalman Gallery.

37. *The Sea.* 1947. Canvas, 45.6 × 61 cm. Private Collection.

38. *Flowers in the Window.* 1956. Canvas, 49.5 × 59.6 cm. H. B. Maitland Collection.

39. *Man Lying on a Wall.* 1957. Canvas, 40.7 × 50.9 cm. Salford Museum and Art Gallery.

40. *Portrait of Anne.* Undated. Board, 35.5 × 25 cm. The L. S. Lowry Estate.

41. *Two Brothers.* 1960. Canvas, 59 × 29.2 cm. Private Collection.

42. *In a Park.* 1963. Canvas, 76.5 × 102 cm. University of Manchester, Whitworth Art Gallery.

43. *Courting.* 1955. Crayon, 26.7 × 36.8 cm. Private Collection.

44. *Four People.* Undated. Panel, 19 × 15.2 cm. The L. S. Lowry Estate.

45. *Bird Looking at Something.* 1964. Board, 16 × 15.6 cm. Collection of Mr Monty Bloom.

46. *The Beggar.* Undated. Board, 19 × 11.4 cm. The L. S. Lowry Estate.

47. *Man Drinking Water.* 1962. Panel, 37.5 × 31.7 cm. Collection of Mr M. D. H. Bloom.

48. *Industrial Scene with Monument.* 1972. Board, 76.2 × 63.5 cm. Private Collection.

1. *Portrait of the Artist's Father.* 1910.
Salford Museum and Art Gallery

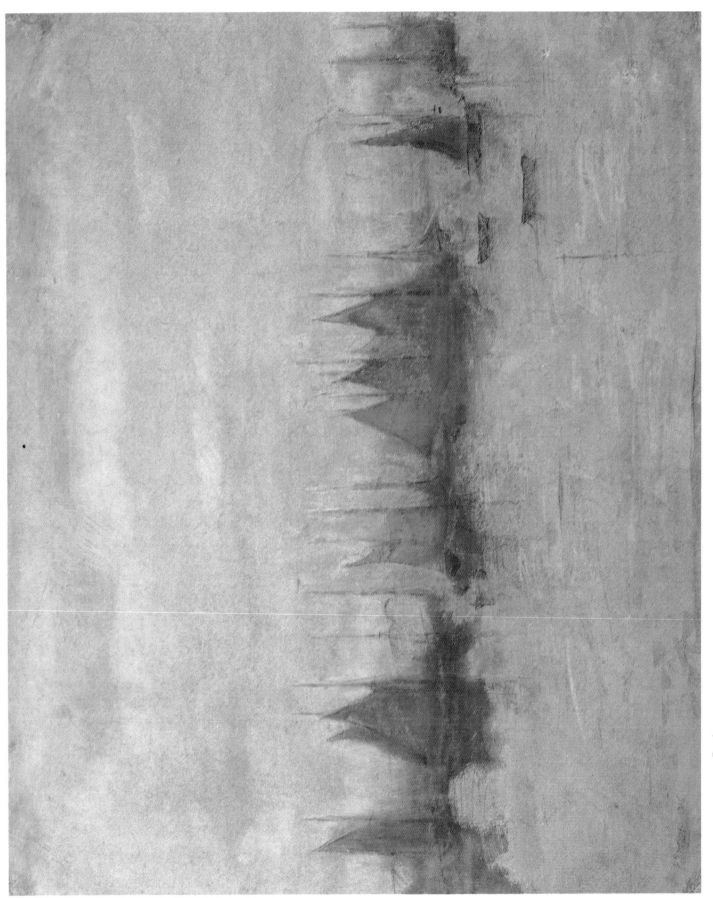

2. *Fishing Boats at Lytham.* 1915.
Collection of Mrs Phyllis Bloom

3. *Bandstand, Peel Park, Salford.* 1928.
Salford Museum and Art Gallery

4. *Peel Park, Salford.* 1927.
Salford Museum and Art Gallery

5. *Pit Tragedy.* 1919.
   Collection of the Revd. Geoffrey S. Bennett

6. *Coming from the Mill.* c.1917–18.
Salford Museum and Art Gallery

7. *Coming from the Mill.* 1930.
Salford Museum and Art Gallery

8.   *The Lodging House*. 1921.
     Salford Museum and Art Gallery

9. *A Quarrel*. 1935.
Collection of Mr Michael Spring

10. *Northern Hospital.* 1926.
Private Collection

11. *Coming out of School.* 1927.
London, Tate Gallery

12. *The Funeral.* 1928.
Collection of Mr Monty Bloom

13. *An Accident.* 1926.
Manchester City Art Galleries

14. *St Augustine's Church, Pendlebury.* 1920.
Collection of the Revd. Geoffrey S. Bennett

15. *Dwellings, Ordsall Lane, Salford.* 1927.
London, Tate Gallery

16. *Returning from Work.* 1929.
Private Collection

17. *Sudden Illness*. 1920.
Collection of Mr M. D. H. Bloom

18. *Self-Portrait*. 1925.
Salford Museum and Art Gallery

19. *The Arrest*. 1927.
Nottingham Castle Museum and Art Gallery

20. *Whit Week Procession at Swinton.* 1921.
Private Collection

21. *Going to the Match*. 1931.
Collection of the Revd. Geoffrey S. Bennett

22. *Sailing Boats.* 1930.
The L. S. Lowry Estate

23.   *The Artist's Bedroom, Pendlebury.* 1940.
Salford Museum and Art Gallery

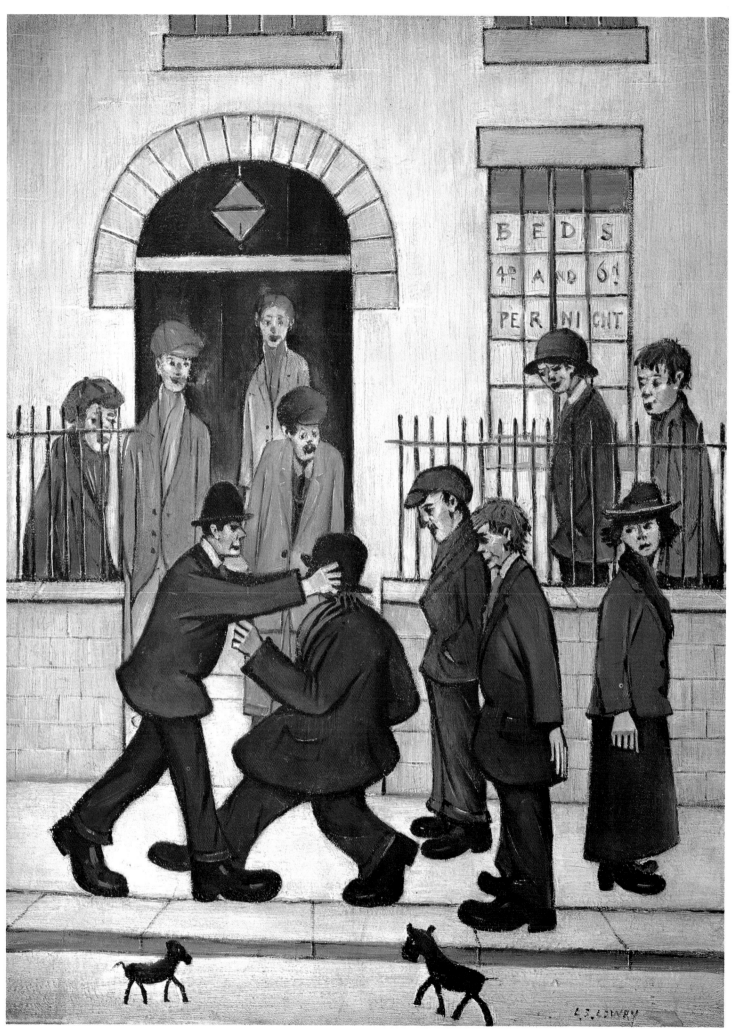

24. *A Fight*. 1935.
Salford Museum and Art Gallery

25. *Head of a Boy in a Yellow Jacket.* 1935.
Collection of Mr M. D. H. Bloom

26. *Landscape in Wigan.* 1925.
Private Collection

27. *St John's Church, Manchester.* 1938.
Collection of the Revd. Geoffrey S. Bennett

28. *Market Scene, Northern Town.* 1939.
Salford Museum and Art Gallery

29. *An Island.* 1942.
Manchester City Art Galleries

30. *A Street Scene, St Simon's Church.* 1928.
Salford Museum and Art Gallery

31. *After the Blitz.* 1942.
Private Collection

32.   *Open Space.* 1950.
London, Crane Kalman Gallery

33.   *Good Friday, Daisy Nook.* 1946.
Private Collection

34. *The Pond.* 1950.
London, Tate Gallery

35. *Lake Landscape.* 1950.
University of Manchester, Whitworth Art Gallery

36. *South Shields.* 1962.
London, Crane Kalman Gallery

37. *The Sea.* 1947.
Private Collection

38. *Flowers in the Window.* 1956.
H. B. Maitland Collection

39. *Man Lying on a Wall.* 1957.
Salford Museum and Art Gallery

40. *Portrait of Anne*. Undated.
The L. S. Lowry Estate

41. *Two Brothers*. 1960.
Private Collection

42. *In a Park*. 1963.
University of Manchester, Whitworth Art Gallery

43. *Courting.* 1955.
Private Collection

44. *Four People*. Undated.
The L. S. Lowry Estate

45. *Bird Looking at Something*. 1964.
Collection of Mr Monty Bloom

46. *The Beggar*. Undated.
The L. S. Lowry Estate

47. *Man Drinking Water*. 1962.
Collection of Mr M. D. H. Bloom

48. *Industrial Scene with Monument.* 1972.
Private Collection